# A Childhood in Ebbw Vale

## a Poetry Anthology

*Dedication to Laura and Sarah*

**by Irene E. Thomas** M.N.F.S.H

Old Bakehouse Publications

© Irene E. Thomas

First published in June 2010

All rights reserved

The right of Irene E. Thomas to be identified as author of this work has been asserted by her in accordance with the Copyright, Designs and Patents Act, 1993.

ISBN 978-1-905967-26-1

Published in the U.K. by
Old Bakehouse Publications
Church Street,
Abertillery, Gwent NP13 1EA
Telephone: 01495 212600  Fax: 01495 216222
Email: theoldbakeprint@btconnect.com
Website: www.oldbakehouseprint.co.uk

Made and printed in the UK
by J.R. Davies (Printers) Ltd.

All rights reserved.
No part of this publication may be reproduced, stored in a retrieval system, or transmitted in any form or by any means, electronic, mechanical, photocopying, recording or otherwise, without the prior permission of the author and/or publishers. For the avoidance of doubt, this includes reproduction of any image in this book on an internet site.

British Library Cataloguing in Publication Data: a catalogue record for this book is available from the British Library.

# Contents

|  | Page |  | Page |
|---|---|---|---|
| About The Author | 4 | Auntie Carrie's Cat | 43 |
| Lullaby | 5 | Monday Memories | 44 |
| Sacrificial Lambs | 6 | Dandelion Time | 45 |
| High Flyer | 8 | Poppies on Gantre | 46 |
| Cold Knap | 10 | School Rocking Horse | 47 |
| Christmas Goose | 12 | Raw Recruit | 48 |
| The Blessed Turkey | 14 | Tea Set | 49 |
| When Gran Lights The Gas | 18 | Dancing Down Cwm | 50 |
| Black Lead | 19 | Brawn | 52 |
| Totting on Gantre | 20 | The Row | 53 |
| Coal Dust Grey | 22 | Red Swimming Costume | 57 |
| Acting Grandmother | 23 | Auntie May | 60 |
| Writing On The Wall | 24 | Picking | 61 |
| Fred Ludlow's War | 25 | Telling the Runes | 62 |
| Moon in a Lucky Bag | 26 | Manmoel | 63 |
| The Pears Soap Picture | 27 | Singer | 64 |
| Sweet Shop | 29 | Winter Wash | 66 |
| Pink Marmite | 31 | Faith | 67 |
| Rags and Bones | 33 | Angels | 68 |
| Taking a Back Pew | 35 | Stained Glass | 69 |
| Rolling Pin | 36 | Search For A Garden | 70 |
| Teachers Marks | 38 | Acknowledgements | 71 |
| White Wash | 41 |  |  |
| Fossilised | 42 |  |  |

# About the Author

Irene E. Thomas was born in Ebbw Vale in 1930. She was educated at the County School and later at Cardiff College of Art from 1947 until 1951.

She has been an Art Teacher, and is a professional freelance artist. Also, she was the Principal of her own School of Dancing for many years, teaching Ballroom, Latin and Old Time and Formation Dancing, as an Associate of the International Dance Teachers Association.

She is a Member of the National Federation of Spiritual Healers, having almost fifty years experience at her own healing centre in Ebbw Vale. Thousands of people were treated here from all over the Country. She is not a member of any religious denomination.

Also, she is a Member of the Welsh Academy, winning many awards as a poet and a writer. Radio Wales has broadcast her poems on *'Pick of the Week'*, and featured her work in individual programmes. As a member of the Arts Council Writers on Tour Scheme she has given many readings to writers groups and visited schools all over Wales, with a residency in Rhymney Comprehensive School.

She won the Cardiff International Welsh Writers Poetry Prize twice, and also First Prize in the Arts Council Competition for Autobiographical Writing for Women in Wales, published by Hoono, also the Oriel Book Prize.

She has also published five volumes of poetry and her work has been featured in various books and magazines, including Poetry Wales and Anglo Welsh Review.

She has written childrens poems published by Pont Books.

# Lullaby

The Sand-man seared my eyes, and fighting to keep them open,
I kicked at the cocoon of flannel, carbolic'd and camphorated.
Worn threads webbed my toes, and bound me to her rhythm.

She paced the kitchen rhyming and rocking,
putting her right foot down as sharply as the chopper
cutting off last men's heads.
Her hand pounded my back,
keeping time with the white faced clock,
where mice ran blindly from the carving.

Falling with Jack and Jill down goose-greased stairs
with an old man, who wouldn't talk to God,
I braced my feet against her arms,
sinewy and hard as the cane, cradling the baby
blown from the bough, broken by wind.

I clawed the sides of her corset,
round as the well and stout as Tommy,
and slid on a wet rubber dummy down a dream of Condensed,
'Unfit for Babies'.
Tired of tantrums, she silenced me with her lullaby,
'Hush, Hush, here comes the bogey man,
he's after little children, he'll catch you if he can,'

I closed my eyes,
hiding from the bogie in the pink-edged dark,
quivering with her endless beating.

# Sacrificial Lambs

I first heard the black ones crying
and learned of their fleecing
as I wet-breathed
through the warmth of their fibres.

They cropped the tip
until cold snaps worried,
and they foraged in Colliers Row,
pawing buckets until they spilled,
grazing ice with clinker and ash.
In the night came the crack of horn on wood
as they rammed shored-up gates,
and shouldered into frozen gardens,
gnawing at stunted stalks and sprouts
solid as a sinker's knuckles.

They sheltered in gulleys between the houses,
and dry-coughed the darkness away.
Stiff and ravenous,
they matted outside half-doors,
heading for curled peelings and outside leaves.

In spite of meagre staple,
came lambs, born on Gantre shale,
and we heard them bleating
for lost mothers and for milk,
and there was no shepherd,
except for the counting and the killing.
In summer, ewes panted under patchy winter coats,
scrubbed skin raw and left woollen shreds
hanging on black tar wires.

The old ones defended against dogs who threatened
and losers made carrion for crows.
Jack-daws,
loud-mouthed keepers of the pecking order,
spread a shivering pall, bruise-black
over common branding and seared flesh.

A few grey hairs remained and a scattering of teeth
worn down with grinding.

They were poor man's meat
and on the chopping block
their heads split
with tempered blade and pounder,
half-brained with steel.
Tongues stilled in aspic.

*Cardiff*
*Literature Festival*
*Wales Writers Prize*

# High Flyer

He wore 'Oxford Bags', and a Fair Isle pullover,
to ape the Prince of Wales
and a cloth cap too big to be called 'Dai'
Even his kite was 'boughten',
an upper class kite,
its tail tied with hard hitting politics from The Times,
pieces of native brown breasts
and bellies from The National Geographic.

Our common kites were made from Co-op
brown paper and saved string,
then given a pasting with flour and water,
tails tied with twists of gossip from
*The News of the World*.

Even the wind, which tore at our home-made kites,
and dashed them to pieces on Gantre tip,
was impressed with this high flyer
and breathed gently on its tightly stretched sides,
dandled it, then sent it soaring.

It took two hands to pull on the stick and
I would have given my right arm to hold it.

Once a year, he unpacked his kite on the bailey
and we followed him up the tip as if we lived in Hamelin,
elbowing each other for a chance carry the tail.

His skin was dark as burned sugar,
tanned with a secret sun lamp,
under which he sprawled on crochet cushions
in his over-stuffed front room.
Sometimes I was ordered to take him
crustless toast,
arranged on a Lipton's tea coupon plate.

When we were alone, he drew me close
to feel the stubble on his chin,
until he grazed my cheeks into fire.
Then tried to kiss it better.

I told God then, that when I was old.
I would crown Mr. 'BIGETTY',
and would not fear a back-hander,
or want to hold his kite.

When I was old enough,
a run-away truck took off his arm,
and I couldn't punch a man with my two
clenched fists,
when he had only one.

# Cold Knap

Only two of us went to Cold Knap,
for she had promised to take me when it was all over.

'Where's the sand, Mam?' I asked.
'Have the Council tipped stones and buried it?'
'Sometimes,' she said, 'there is no soft ground.'

She spread her thin black coat over the pebbles
and it hurt, for she had made a hard bed to lie on.
My sleeves were circled with cotton bands,
stab-stitched with respect.

I took off my shirred elastic cotton dress, patterned
with wreaths of forget-me-nots on a muddy ground.
Underneath, I was plain'd and pearl'd
into a knitted costume, caught in chains and strands
she had woven between her sharp needles.

The grey edge of the sea
slapped my legs as if it was all my fault.
Water sucked back over the pebbles as noisily as Auntie Bet,
with a Fisherman's Friend between her dentures
on a Sunday in Bethesda,
and me in an aura of chlorodyne and unforgiven sin.

The pebbles moved underfoot
and I slid down a steep trough into the sea.
I lost sight of Mam and screamed at the separation,
until she hauled me back,
costume sagging with the weight of water.
She hit out and thumped me for being unharmed.

I wanted to take home the pebbles in my tin bucket,
cartoon'd with Mickey Mouse,
but there was no laughter in the day.
'Leave them.' she ordered,
'the burden gets heavier the longer you bear it,
and I cannot carry any more.'

I dropped the stones one by one, marking where I had been,
white stones without epitaph.

One left, I put it on the garden wall,
with only shale and cinder for company,
pale-cheeked in a heat wave
without the familiar touch of the sea
to bring back the colour.

# Christmas Goose

Downstairs,
I had heard of the Gander
and the violence.

I watched
the annual pantomime of goose feathers,
the hissing and the cackling.

My Grandmother, knee deep in down,
plucked the Christmas goose.
Feathers flew from her fingers,
cushioned the wooden chairs,
and settled a white cover on the table.

I clapped my hands
and the feathers danced to set patterns
over the oiled cloth,
a ballet along familiar lines.

They hung in the air
and with a sharp intake,
filled my mouth until I spat out.
I stuffed armfuls into bolsters
and pillows cased in ticking.
Up to my elbows in warm snow,
I chilled.

The pimples
and the comic appearance of the stripped bird
gave rise to old chestnuts.
'His goose is cooked',
drew ribald laughter-come-to-crying.

Upstairs
on chesty nights,
I slipped into goose-greased dreams,
held between the bony knees of nightmare.

White winged sheets
beat like angels guarding,
as my Grandfather played his part
with the cutting edge,
and circled the long white neck
of Mother Goose
with a gash of ruby.
I buried my face in the pillow
to deaden the screaming and the song,
but feathers suffocated.

# The Blessed Turkey

Said Gran,
'We're out of luck.
There won't be chicken or a duck
for Christmas Day!.
I can't believe it's Christmas Eve.
It really is the end.
I pray to God to help,
and if he can't come Himself, to send.'

Heaven sent, Uncle Jim staggered in,
a huge sack on his back,
dumped it on the table, 'Crack'.
'That,' he said, 'is our Christmas dinner.'
'My lucky number came up a winner.'
Said Auntie Ade.
'Paid a penny for a raffle in Nantyglo,
and what do you know ? We won.'
'No. Never' said Gran, 'You're making fun,
It's a joke - or a pig.'
and she gave it a poke.

'Stand back' said Jim, and whipped off the sack.
Couldn't believe what we saw with our eyes.
A tremendous turkey. It was first prize!.
'Oh God, it's a beauty,' Grancher said,
'but then, everybody's lovely after they're dead'.

'It's a blessing.' said Gran, 'there is no doubt.'
'Stop messing about.
I'll soon have all its innards pulled out.'
She mixed up sage and onion stuffing,
blowing and puffing
'We'll need a miracle to fill this bird,' she said.
'I've already used up five loaves of bread.'
'Gran,' I said, 'God's made a muck'
'That's not a turkey he's sent, It's a duck.'
She stuck in a fork.

'Don't talk so simple.'
'Well, why is it covered with all those goose pimples?.'

'Half a mo !', said Gran
'Its too big for my pan or baking tin
and our oven's too small.
It won't go in backwards or forwards at all.
We'll do it old fashioned on the spit.
Turn and baste it bit by bit.'
It took all Christmas Day to cook.
We dined like posh people in Badminton Grove.
Dinner late at half past eight.
Ate till we bust, the neighbours too,
the dog next door and our cat.
'Whew, don't fancy any more of that.' said Mam.
'Mustn't waste,' Gran replied.
We had it all ways, baked, grilled and fried.
Had it cold and hot, boiled in stew,
minced, brawned and rissoled too.

We'd had our fill and the neighbours as well,
the dog next door ran like a gazelle,
when he heard us call, and the cat
scrabbled away up the garden wall.
It beat all, for a cat to run from a bird.
Our next door neighbours
kept their doors shut tight.
'There's more turkey'. Gran had to shout.
They heard allright,
but they wouldn't come out.

'I know,' said Gran, 'I'll make a tart'.
'Don't start' said Ade, 'we've had a feed.
'I need a pill,' said Jim, 'I'm feeling ill.
I've got the hots, and the turkey trots.'
'Let's go Ade' Jim said, 'quick as we can'
'I'll make you sandwiches to take back' said Gran,
'with plenty of salt.'
Uncle Jim lost his turkey.

He swore to Gran, on his next weeks dole,
it wasn't his fault.
The way home was murky, he tripped,
and the turkey fell out of the sandwiches
down a coal hole.

On New Year's Eve as Gran went to bed
'I'll make soup from the bones tomorrow' she said.
Grancher groaned
'I've had a belly full of this he moaned,
burned the carcass up the tip.

'Where's that blessed turkey gone? said Gran
'It's risen again out of the pan,
gone to the farmyard in the sky
where all good turkeys go after they die
flown to the other side of the track.
The only thing is 'oops' it keeps coming back.'

Now I never eat turkey,
can't stand the stuff.
for I remember the day when
we had too much
and yet, there was not enough.

*Jim and Emily Selway,*
*Colliers Row, 1930.*
*Grandfather and Grandmother*

*The Kitchen, Colliers Row.*

# When Gran Lights The Gas

When we have used up all the daylight and it gets too dark to see, Gran lights the gas. She is only a twt, so she climbs up on the armchair and kneels on the table to reach the tap.

She turns the gas on, it hisses out of the mantle and smells of dirty socks. To get down quick, she puts her leg out backwards off the table and tries to find the mat with her toe. Sometimes her slipper falls off or catches in her long black skirts and then her tongue clicks.

When she gets to the fire, she climbs up on to the steel fender to reach for a spill from the blue jug, decorated with a picture of a windmill. It would be easier if she kept the jug on the window-sill, but Gran won't have anything moved if it has been there a long time.

Every Sunday she and Grancher make spills from the *News of the World*. They cut long strips, wet their thumbs and roll the paper into tight stalks. It saves using matches. Gran says that it is wasteful to use matches when we have a fire.

She rams the spill into a burning coal and then holding the paper down to catch, carries it back to the mantle. She climbs on to the chair and the table again and bits of burned paper fall on to the oilcloth. I blow them away and they fly like jackdaws.

Sometimes the flame is douted down to sparks.

'Drat the thing,' says Gran and starts all over again.

When she puts the flame to the mantle, I screw up my eyes and there is a loud bang. The mantle spits to green and Gran's white eyebrows go a bit brown and curl.

She won't have electric light, like Mrs. Harry down the Row. Gran says 'Electricity is dangerous.'


*(Extract from her prize winning essay in the book 'ON MY LIFE', published by 'Honno', the Welsh Women's Press, in 1989.)*

# Black Lead

It was all blacking,
every day of our Cherry-Blossomed, boot-licking lives.
Bar-shoes and brogues with laces crossed for luck,
irons, doorstops and fenders.

Polishing fire bricks and slates into mirrors,
dark enough to ask who was the fairest.
Even wished we could polish the night
to reflect in the Ty Bach.
We climbed the garden path and in our cupped hands,
the tallow flame died.
The night edged round in memorial,
black as the stinking stumbling back alley
and the twelve-o-clock front road,
running dark as senna,
after mean-fisted street lights dowted.
We slept under an icy pitch of slates,
in bedrooms, black as tar.

In the cold knee-cracking morning,
acrid-black lead smeared our breath
filled the kitchen like sal-volatile,
but ashes risen, we knew the satisfaction of burnished brass
and clean boots on the top step, their polished-apple toes
ready to kick the day.

*Published in Poetry in Wales*

# Totting On Gantre

A warning cry
from the man working out his seven weeks on the council,
and pieces of people's lives cascaded from the tip-up lorry,
down the sides of Gantre tip.

We elbowed each other, totting for treasures
and our feet sank in ash and clinker
which filled darned socks and seg-heavy shoes.

Dark blue bottles pungent with liniment,
pop bottles, throttled with a green glass marble,
rolled down to our feet.
A fragment of ribbon plate with a transfer of roses, delighted,
and a piece of willow pattern with two lovers running away,
deserved some spit to make it clean.
A china head from a sightless doll drew shudders,
but I cradled it
in the skirt of the dress Auntie Jane had made.
From its shirred waist streamed flowers in black stripes
which reminded me of mourning.

On the concrete cap of Gantre shaft,
we played house and fried slices of thin grey shale
in a cack-handed pan until they smelled of bacon.
Keys, uncurled from fins where sardines had lain
top to tail in their oily beds
as we did among goose feathers,
opened spaces left for doors.

We spread newspaper cloths printed with a crumpled
Mrs. Simpson and a Duke losing face,
then laid out our finds.
Half a plate for half a crust,
and half a cup for half an Oxo.
We hard-boiled stones in washer-weary saucepans
and set them in egg cups
printed with a cracked Kitchener,
who had pointed the way to France
where my grandfather picked up pieces of men.

On our common brick mantelpiece we set ornaments,
a boy with legs gone from under,
a kicked-in brass boot,
a Peace Mug with a crazed Britannia,
and an alarm clock
with hands stopped at nineteen-thirty-five.

# Coal Dust Grey
(Colliers Row 1930)

Washing
billowing across the bailey.
Shirts and spencers,
combinations,
merging into coal dust grey.

Turn the mangle,
pound the dolly.
Wooden pegs dance on the line,
sheets and blankets
turned to middle,
patched and washed a coal
dust grey.

Baby clothes,
their pristine whiteness
hanging short
on rusty lines,
cradled in the grimy breezes,
growing into coal dust grey.

'Quick it's raining',
grab the washing,
joust the prop, wind in the line.
Make your Mam
a living clothes horse,
saddled with the coal dust grey.

Pit and mangle, move together,
married in an endless motion.
Starch and blue-bag,
pick and shovel,
turning love
a coal dust grey.

*Broadcast on Radio Wales*

# Acting Grandmother

She never drew back the curtain,
only half-appeared
in the spotlight of my searching questions.

Once, she let me reach out
and curl my fingers round her hand-span waist.
She was hard and rigid as a Russian doll,
her peasant costume,
a sacking apron splayed over a skirt in black-out rep.

I marvelled at her magic,
conjuring quilts from patches and scraps,
and crochet lace from invisible thread.
She changed dandelions and nettles to wine,
bottling up a sunburst on the tongue, a sting around the edges.

Without prompting,
she never dried on Catechism, Psalm or Creed,
and sometimes chanted old Music Hall songs,
rhythmic, but tuneless, and almost came through,
remembering stars.

I often watched the nightly performance
as she high-stepped out of her petticoats,
gathering up the flannel bouquet of Wintergreen and Fiery-Jack.

Holding in, she unhooked her stays,
shored with whalebone, and keeping to routine,
loosened her puckered shimmy.
It was lined with Thermogene,
tacked in each winter and worn until Hawthorn was out.

Under cover, she threw up her arms in a final gesture
and the wincyette gown she slept in
wreathed around her bowed shoulders.

I missed her, when the curtains closed.

# Writing On The Wall

The stones were curved and rhubarb red,
on the top of the wall.
We sat astride sailing the Queen Mary
and driving to Barry Island.
In our own cars.

With slivers of slate, we scratched lover's names
and sent arrows through broken hearts.
'Wyndham loves Violet
Dereck loves Violet
Violet loves Mervyn Price

and 'Vote Vote for 'Neurin Bevan.'

Made a drawing of Maggie Davies
fag stuck to her lip,
Patty Mason, head white with nits.
Shirley Temple, and Billy Prosser with
his sunken glass eye.

We chalked nick-names and rude names.
Olwen Parry was dirty,
drew two dots for eyes, one for a belly-button.
We rubbed it out so that nobody could see.
Scratched children with crooked legs,
stick men and women with holes for eyes.
Houses in rows, with windows in corners,
chimneys with scribble for smoke,
clouds on horizons,
paths leading nowhere.

# Fred Ludlow's War

After standing for King and Country, an invasion of picture-goers
from the Palace and the White House
charged into the perishing night and down the hill to Fred's,
where the smell of frying chips
spread a warm blessing, between Libanus and the Prims.
Ammunition ready, Fred served in his striped shirt,
his bald head shining like the domed covers of his pans.
Tails and cutlets, coated with flour,
dropped delicately from his nicotined fingers,
floated in boiling oil until the skin blistered.
'Mrs.' Ludlow, the evacuee,
doled out Cockney with the Cod and the crackling
and hair-raising stories of the Blitz.
Her permanent, a shock around her face.
The daughter leaned provocatively over the counter
making fish-eyes at the exempt and the medically unfit,
getting an eye-full of her see-through blouse, in spite of steam.
At first, bullies and agressors elbowed to the front
and demanded their three penny-worth.
Small-fry went to the wall.
Then we joined up and queued for equal rations,
lined the wooden counter,
where the scrubbed grain stood to attention.
Spread over news, dark stains blotted out Dunkirk.
The salty liquid soaked through and under battering,
soldiers tore.
We were too young to serve but while we waited our turn,
we drank Fred's vinegar, and he played war with us.

*Published in Poetry Wales*

# Moon in a Lucky Bag

In Fairy tales,
they say that when you know the name of a spirit,
power is diminished, the hold weakened
and the fear.

We waited for his coming as if he were Messiah.
At the appointed time between two and five,
he appeared at the Bargoed Emporium.
It was all jingle, and dreams wrapped in paper parcels.
A Tooth Fairy
who could fill an aching gap with silver,
waved her wand over the coinage
and sent it to Toyland on overhead wires.

I sat in his red lap, harder than I had imagined,
in an aura of humbug and told him my name.
He asked for a kiss and promised me the moon in a lucky bag.

When they told me, I cried in disbelief,
then I recalled the dish-pan hands of the fairy,
his bony knees and the peppermint breath.

I had often seen him slumped on a seat in the Old Man's Park,
disguised in a Dai-cap and long greasy mac,
watching children swinging on the Witches Hat,
and offering his hot breath sweets.

# The Pears Soap Picture

In winter,
darkness came down early to the kitchen,
where mean windows doled out their daily pittance of light.
Gran sat on the scrubbed wooden bench,
she had ingrained with carbolic, making a mat.
She pegged remnants of an old coat
into sacking, humped over her knees,
pinching and pulling through the cut pieces,
and piling them into a ragged border,

The Pears Soap Picture hung above the mantel-piece,
its glass, fly spotted, and sooty in corners,
where the duster had not reached.

Our fire was low and I was very cold
so, I walked in the garden of the Pears Soap picture,
between stone pillars leading to a desert,
where sun warmed to the bone,
and envied the lady lying on satin pillows in Persia,
for behind her, perfumed peacock feathers fanned hot air,
and a carpet spread along the wall,
its ancient patterns woven with jewel colours,
amethyst, garnet and emerald.
It was a magic carpet, on which to feel my feet and fly.

It was too dark to see clearly, but looking into the glass,
I knew that one day, I would buy scented soap,
tread on softer ground and live in the warm.

*Reproduced with kind permission of Dr. M. Chadda.*

# Sweet Shop

The flavour of liquorice reminded me.
Coiled around a mauve sweet,
bought for a penny from Parry's shop,
on the corner of Western Terrace.

Windows, blinded with adverts,
Mazawattee Tea, Hovis and Robin Starch.
Soako and Swan Soap made the shop dark in corners
where old potatoes pushed dry roots into damp sacks.

We rubbed our noses against the glass,
tongues pretending to taste jelly babies,
wine gums, coconut tobacco and aniseed balls.
Wished we had a penny for a bar of 'Five Boys',
or a pink sugar mouse with a real string tail.
Envied David Bowen, cheek gumboiled with a gob stopper,
a sweet cigarette stuck to his lip.

Mr. Parry,
hemmed in with cards of needles, hooks and eyes,
Back and Kidney pills, dummies, Ex-lax and Ipecacuanha,
grasped coins with nicotine fingers, restless for a Woodbine
Pale against a rainbow of bottles, waistcoat buttons straining,
he tipped yellow sherbet into paper cones,
counting every grain.

The smell of fish on Tuesday lingered on iron scales,
freshened with boiled ham on Wednesdays,
but Fridays, after school, wafts of home-made toffee,
setting round green apples drew us in.

Mr. Parry made us stay outside,
fingering the small brown stones on his pebble-dashed wall,
wishing they were sweets.

*Pink Marmite*

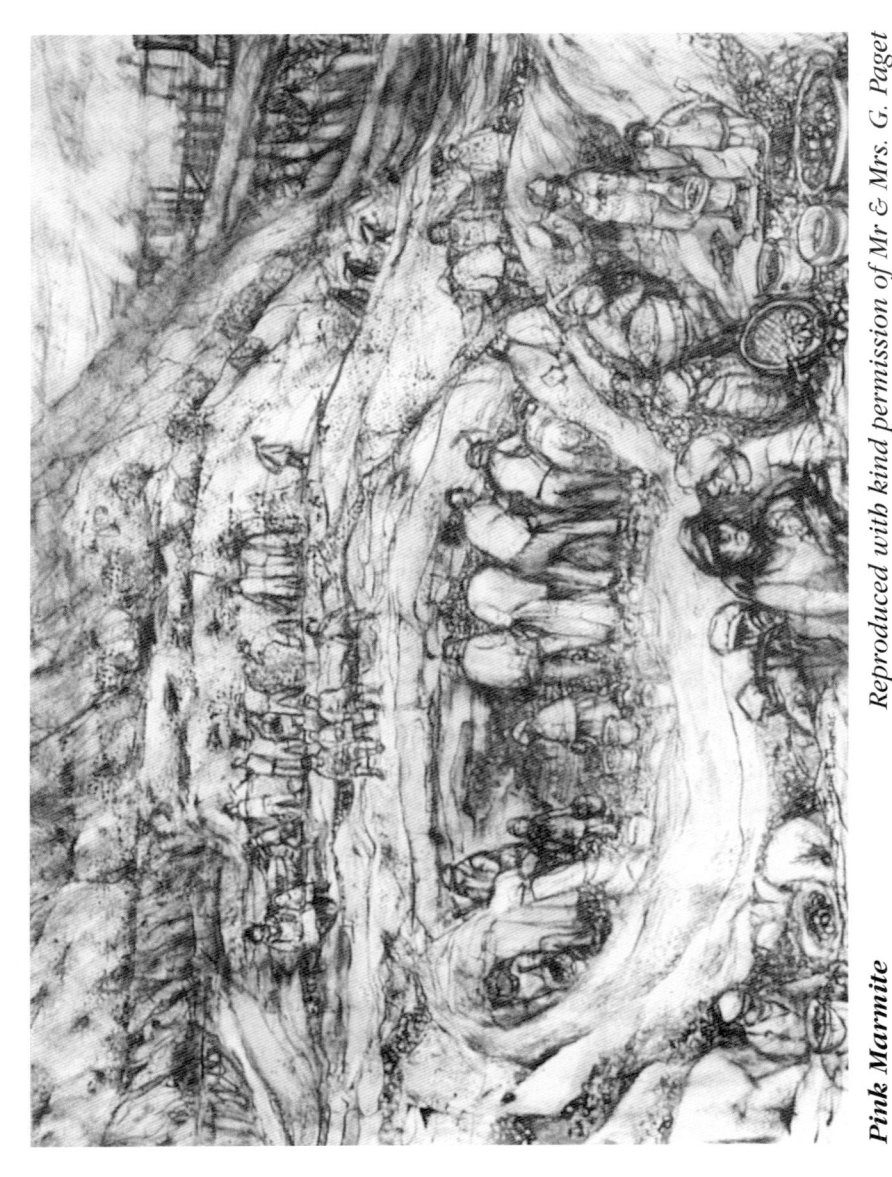

*Reproduced with kind permission of Mr & Mrs. G. Paget*

*"She saw it on film - picking coal on the slag heaps"*

# Pink Marmite

We did not know then about her,
not having read the Romances,
the affairs of Lords and Ladies
and their decorous love-making.

Our set had not heard of Cartland Pink,
for we were socially acceptable in hand-me-downs
patched in brown and grey and black.

We had seen stars,
the sequins and the satin and the peroxided hair.
watched open-mouthed when we saw them
and the food on the tables which they never seemed to eat.

She saw us on film in black and white,
picking coal on the slag heaps,
and rickety babies wrapped in clouds of coal dust,
and the men with hollow cheeks.
Under chiffon and lace, her heart beat as strongly
as one of her heroines when she saw the handsome Duke.

The Cartland pink is now gone,
but we remember her kindness.
She sent us vitamin B, bottles of Marmite for the starving,
but she did not see through her rose coloured spectacles,
that we did not have bread to spread it on.

*Rags and Bones*

*Reproduced with kind permission of Mr. & Mrs. G. Paget*

# Rags and Bones

This scrap-heap of a man
bellowed through a tin bugle
in his own ragged rhythm.

He changed old threads into farthings and oriental fish.
and we gathered round his cart to see shining scales of carp,
swimming in jam jars from the Co-op.

Streaks of gold, open-mouthed and gulping
at the skin-tight surface of a raspberry pip sea.

He carted bones in the sacking, sheep's heads, without brains
and shoulders broken with bearing heavy burdens,
to be made into glue for things which become unstuck

'Can I have some rags, Mam?' I begged
She said
'Sorry love, we're wearing them.'

*A Bit of Luck*

# Taking a Back Pew

In chapel, it's all backs and cold shoulders,
scarf ends and Mrs Morgan's plastic mac,
sticking to the pew.
It is satin suns of bald heads
rising from the Gadair Fawr,
powderings of dandruff, straying hairs and hats.

Sir behind the hat of Mrs. Parry
gift wrapping the preacher in a brown ribbon bow,
dull as his sermon.
Feathers tickle his ribs, like Eve to Adam,
never sees the funny side.
Sit behind Mrs. Evans
filling the rostrum with Harvest Festival,
artificial cherries and sour grapes.
Oliver Jacob,
Housing Allocation Officer, sidesman, collar greasy as his palm
and Susan Phillips, her fiery hair
tempting a young man to burn his fingers.
Auntie Et's is down to ash,
rolled in steel, set on edge
around the brim of her hat,

It is pimples erupting on Billy Probert's neck
standing up to be counted,
red ears, and Lily Mansen's transparent blouse,
her black bra cutting into flesh across her back
deep as the valley of the shadow.

Mrs. Jenkins is dying to sit, soldering on
with her replacement hip.
"Stand up, stand up for Jesus",
and pregnant Mary Probert, sorry for sinning,
prays for the sweep
to come to her wedding,
so that she can touch him
for a bit of luck.

# Rolling Pin

It is the colour of warm gingerbread,
an old tool, oiled with suet and loose lard,
scorch-marked from the griddle and the baking.

Eyes level with the edge of the table,
I watched its easy wooden handles rotate under her fists,
four bone moons, pushing an ocean of pastry,
making waves which fanned out into a spume of Self-Raising.
She hoisted pastry on to the pin like a sail, and dredging,
slapped it down full bellied on the board.

She rolled to even thickness,
and when it lay flat as spilled milk,
she stamped out rounds with serrated edges,
and laid them over black holes of patty tins,
indented with stars and shells.
I saw the soft white circles
sag under the weight of Golliwog Raspberry,
delicately scraped off a tea spoon with her little finger.

Rolling up,
she tented over chunks of cooking apple pie,
and sometimes over wild bramble and whinberry.
Her hand spread beneath the enamel plate,
and she spun it on the edge of a knife, cutting a perfect ring,
then forked a frill around the edges, to tart.
I begged for left overs,
Wound the trimmings and cut-work
into a loose baji and rolled to transparency.
Pastry cat-cradled from my fingers,
and fell into slow elastic holes.
The pin was never washed.
'Makes it stick,' she said,
and coaxed it clean with a damp cloth and a dusting,
then hung it from its string,
stiff with flour on its own six inch nail in the pantry.

Sometimes, she used it as a weapon,
always promising, especially to my Grandfather,
home late from the Con. Club
stumbling against the front room furniture in the dark.
His shame-face glowed through the half opened middle door
and with a mumbled 'Go' night Em',
he disappeared into the back bedroom,
without his supper of tongue pie.

Now, when I reach for her belaying pin,
with an urge to flatten.
I remember how she spared the rod,
and smoothed over,
with a cool hand and a light touch.

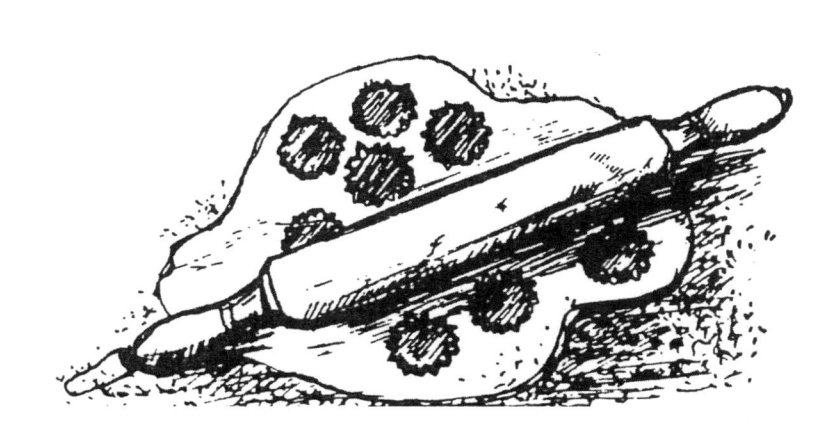

# Teachers Marks

Ink tattoos my finger a mark from Pontygof
where the yard put it's arm round the classroom
held me in at playtime.
I hop-scotched, ran, skipped, dipped.
'Olika Bolika, Soup and Solika, Olika Bolika, Knob.'
'You're On 'It', 'No, Not fair,' 'I was 'It' last time.'

Miss Peck, Head mistress. smaller than me,
the biggest person I knew, after God.
There was silence where she walked,
her whispers reached the farthest corners,
dried our mouths, held our tongues.

There were wafts of wet knickers,
carbolic soap, damp coats cooking on iron radiators.
Milk spurting from holes centred in cardboard tops.
We hated Amos, the Nit Nurse, with her purple ointment,
pulling up our vests behind the blackboard,
to see if our mothers were clean.

Patty Morgan reeked.
Her mother replied to a note on hygiene
'I do send my Patty to school to be teached, not smelt.'

Miss Doughton,
full bodied, voice and bosom to match,
rolled out the cracked parchment charts.
flung them over the board.

'Doh me soh doh. Doh soh me doh.'
She sang 'Hen Wlad Fy Nhadau' and 'Rise, rise thou merry Lark'.
Her shattering soprano embraced our uncertain solfa,
vibrated the windows
where the cracked panes caught their breath

Heads on desks!
Breathing in hot polish, dried ink and stale pepsin,
stuck underneath,
breathing out wet patches to draw in.
Shifting, scraping shoes, pulling socks,
Blowing into a circus of dust tumbling in shafts of sun.

I liked Miss Stevens best.
Gaunt, nervous, her hair grey as men's socks.
Sometimes her voice stretched to a tight shriek,
cleaned the board afterwards, to hide her face,
but when she read, I heard the music,
opened my inner eye, saw the host of daffodils,
the ten thousand dancing.
Waves of yellow washed on shores I had yet to tread.

Miss Stevens never used the cane, but left her mark in me.

**White Wash**
*painting by Irene Thomas
reproduced with kind permission of Mrs. Joan Smith*

# White Wash

It covered the face of Colliers Row,
a parched skin, cracking and flaking.

When light nights showed up red ash from Bessemer,
deposits of grey basic slag,
and the contents of chamber pots dashed over the walls,
suddenly it was time.
It was decided as surely as the law,
which changed skipping to whipping-top or jackstones
to marbles.

One whitewashed front appeared,
like a new false tooth in a grin of nicotine,
then whitewash fever raged down the Row
and women came out in a rash of rag-and-bone jumpers,
crossover pinnys, and worn Whitson daps,

Limestone, burned in the kilns at Llangattwg,
sucked thirstily at tap water in tin baths
and old hard bass-brooms stirred in scalding lime,
losing a few more bristles.

Slapping and sloshing,
they white-washed the lav at the top of the gardens
painting stones to point the way,
sent white water rapids down green slimed drains,
and plastered back bailey walls,
tide-marked with last years grime.

There were no jobs for men in this annual circus,
but women worked like clowns with common good humour
with red eyes smarting and drawn white mouths.

# Fossilised

We played on the concrete cap of the pit shaft,
building half-brick houses and corner shops,
cemented with muck and gobs of imagination.
Secret doors opened with keys from sardine tins
where plaited fish had swum in oil.
In that daydream, we did not know then
that there were other creatures underfoot,
where the wind still sighed for company in empty galleries,
and the sea had whispered
and sand softly covered Spirobis and Estheria,
names foreign to our valley tongue.

They were older than great grandfather,
who sat rigid in the slow eye of the camera,
holding his breath, in the strangle-hold of a white collar
and the Sunday torture of front and back studs.
Older than great grandmother, framed in sepia,
with set lips and buttoned-up bosom,

Older than Gran, her hair scraped back to glory,
face crazed with crevices where anger lived.
Older than her potato knife, honed down to a sliver of steel,
slicing like her sharp words through daftness.
Memory is imprinted now
with patterns deeply etched, and in this age,
I think it was a kindness
that I did not know then what 'old' was.

# Auntie Carrie's Cat

Dark as midnight without moon,
he watched with one yellow eye,
squinting through the other,
half-closed with an old scar.
His joints, once well oiled,
now dry as a licked out sardine tin,
made slinking difficult.
In the autumn of his ninth life,
he could still spit, spat and box.
Ginger Jenkins from the Old Boot Inn
knew the sharpness of his left and right hooks.

On clear nights,
when the voices of the Cwm Dyffryn Choir
scaled roofs and clung round cowls
and cracked chimneys in Cwm,
he out-howled them, his tongue trembling in a feline falsetto.

He sang
of the alley where Mrs. Jones
threw the vinegared skins of her Friday haddock,
chip-shop papers,
smacking of cod and crackling,
unpicked tailbones and fried fins,
chicken livers, wingless birds,
and goldfish, gasping in glass globules
on the Rag and Bones Man's cart.

On Sundays,
in the warm after-dinner kitchen,
whiskers washed and slicked,
he challenged the china lions
and put them in their place on the mantelpiece.
Then, stretching into a long forgetting,
he sprang into the cradle of Auntie Carrie's lap,
settled his bones into a soft circle under her soothing hands
and slowly closed his good eye.

# Monday Memories

She rarely said the word, or showed it.
I was underfoot, so moved away
while she carried from the cwch,
benches, the iron boiler
tin baths and brass scrubbing board.

I lost her in suds and steam.
Sheets wound over her arms,
clung around her neck as she wrung out.
On the line, they tugged at taught wire,
puckered up, sucked wet kisses,
clung to each other, pulling away with a smack.
They touched her gently,
as she set the prop against the line like an arrow.

'I love' she said, 'To see them blow on a good day'.
When they were dry, she filled her arms,
warmed, uncooked, tucked them in.
Afterwards she was too tired.

*Monday Memories*
*reproduced with kind permission of Mr. & Mrs G. Paget*

44

# Dandelion Time

We bunched the milky hollows of their stems
and thrust them into rusty cans
to decorate half brick houses
cemented with muck and gobs of imagination.
Pee-the-beds, pulled from overlays of shale,
were stirred in stews of lazy daisies
in a cack-handed pan.

When their sun had changed to moon,
we blew on them to tell the time
one o'clock, two o'clock, three o'clock, four,
not counting days or measuring hours.
They spiralled from our fingers
to circle wind in summer snow.
They rode on flanks of ponies, until out of puff
flocked old Sammy's beard
and the ticking on his mattress
where he slept, come opening time.

On the tip edge,
Wyndham Parry,
tired of asking daisies,
blew down soft kisses
to his love in Colliers Row.

# Poppies On Gantre

Outcasts,
thrown clear of the confines of a wedlock of wire,
sowing wild seed in dry ash,
they grew rampant as docks and dandelions.

They felt the drumming of the valley wind,
burst through brittle shale
and in the carnival of the morning, paraded,
striped and black busby'd, brash as young jazz bands.

Their buds, easy in embryonic sleep,
nodded and swayed to music half-remembered
but we ripped their green bellies with sharp-edged nails,
underlined with Gantre grime.
Hooked out folded frills and un-ironed skirts,
made them dance to our beating until they dropped
and left them gutted, purple and pink,
on Gantre.

# School Rocking Horse

Dappled moons rose and fell,
shone in glossy varnish,
and under his horse-hair,
wild glass eyes glinted.
I circled him, this painted mountain pony,
linked as if there was a rope between
and he breaking me.
Once, I dared to touch his nostril
and the red paint flared and burned.
I curled my finger back into my palm,
recoiled from chomping teeth
and the stretched mouth.

His ears pricked, yet stopped
to rhymes of fine ladies and rings
and the cries to be excused
and the sing-song.

I did not put up my hand to be chosen,
for when he took the bit, he bucked.
His luminous eye was fixed on a distance,
where a yard was a million miles,
and he would not stop,
impatient for anther crack of the whip.

He was old then and his breed ancient.
First carved in clay and thrown in terra cotta,
then flanked with sanded beechwood and mahogany.
His ancestors, gaudy pole-horses,
prancing on barley-sugar brass,
fair-ground gallopers, jibbers and racers,
'Prince' and 'Wonder', 'Nib' and 'Dobbin'.

I rode this Hobby Horse
and gave the runaway his head.
Gripped the piebald flanks with shaking knees,
until he slowed and the creaking stopped.

# Raw Recruit

Rain polished the pewter street, outside the Citadel.
It washed away the Saturday suns
chalked on the pavement by the old soldier,
drawing dreams of Summer Lands.
His chalk white ships, sank in a concrete sea.
They beat the drum, and it drew me in,
out of the wet night into the Sunshine Hour.
It was light and music brass-bright and toe-tapping.
Recruits, badged and bonnet-ed,
buttoned up and bursting, sang and clapped,
fighting the Good Fight.
Clashing tambourines, skin-tight,
tapped on elbows and knees, ribbons flying,
and faces red with effort and the gladness of it all.
Volunteering, I climbed the steps.
The Captain held me up above the rostrum
and I sang, of a bird, and how God had taught it to fly.
Still in the Light,
I ran home down the dark tunnel of the back bailey,
 forgetting bogey-men, head full of Good News and Hallelujahs.
'I'm going to join the Army, Mam,'
'You' she said, pouring cold water,
'are in the Wesleyans, and there you'll stay!.'

I had not been near the war,
but knew I was already a prisoner.

# Tea Set

Our common cups were all odds and nothing matched.
It was rag-and-bone china,
the thick-lipped earthenware pieces,
had cracks in the glazing
which showed up the poverty of the material.
We drank our tea down to dregs
which afterwards damped down the small.

Our best set was put by,
wrapped carefully in 'The Chronicle'
and only brought out for visitors.
This superior set,
with side dishes wreathed in rose-buds,
was laid out on a dead-white cloth,
rigid with Robin Starch.
When Uncle Bill came to tea,
he spoke Cardiff posh and puffed out from his pipe
a blessing in a cloud of Balkan Sobrani.

He stirred a sharp tongued slice of lemon into his beverage
and we managed wry smiles.

It was polite bread and butter first,
and no mucking in to the boughten sponge,
no burping or slurping and we drank
with little fingers up in the world.

# Dancing Down Cwm

Between the mountains Manmoel and Cefn Yr Arael,
streets hold hands,
making chains along the railway lines.
Rusty trucks nudge each other, noisily,
like adolescent boys, sharing a dirty joke.
Pulled, shunted, cajoled into Marine Colliery,
where hoppers fill their grimy mouths with coal.

Houses subside, struggle to support each other,
lean and whisper their repeating patterns,
"Door window window chimney,
door window window chimney!"
Tell the secrets of the front rooms and back kitchens
and the gossip brought from
Tyllwyn, Victoria and Waunlwyd,
by the garrulous River Ebwy.

The night sidles down the street,
recoils from the open doors of the members' bars
of 'The Con Club', 'The Sailors', 'The Legion'
and 'The Riverside'.

Up the drunken stairway,
a notice, 'FOR MEN ONLY'.
a class, held by my father, a dancer, in Cwm.

Down in Marine, men pick, shovel, slide, sway,
keep their balance on the rough pit bottom,
cobbled with coal, crossed by railway lines.
Wipe sweat from their eyes, ringed with coal dust.
Teeth fluorescent in the dark,
minstrels in a grimy performance.
In the upper room
heavy boots stamp, learners recite,
'One two three, one two three'.
'Is it right foot to start?'
Red handkerchiefs mop heads damp with sweat.
'The trouble is, I can do it lovely by myself,
but when I get holt of our May, she puts her foot

right where I want to put mine.
Left two three, right two three.
Eyes glued on my father's feet,
gliding over the French chalk,
dancing
The Valeta,
The Waltz
and the Tango Fascination.

Earnestly plodding,
Billy Thomas dances a duel with Tommy Parsons
Holding on to each other like drowning men,
desperate to learn the Quickstep by Saturday.
Hoping they can ask Mary Penry for a dance,
after the match
up The Betterment.

Next door,
in the throes of her fifth labour,
Ida Solway hears the noise,
groans and perspires,
pulls on the towel, looped over the iron bedstead
and blesses her husband
dancing the Two Step with my father, in Cwm.

Auntie Carrie,
paper thin, asthma wracked,
warm as colliers coal,
hangs on to her fire-guard,
draped with damp washing, wishes she could breathe again
and go dancing.

Uncle Herb
sits on the red plush sofa,
with the stuffing coming out of the back
takes off his celluloid leg
and the padded ring that gives him 'gyp'
curses the run-a-way dram
which stopped him dancing
with my father, in the Con. Club
down Cwm.

# Brawn

Every night, Gran cooks something from nothing, but when Gran makes brawn, the house stinks all day.

She buys her pig's heads from Tommy Lloyd, the butcher. He lines them up in his window and stuffs oranges in their mouths. Gran gets the orange free.

She forks out the pig's eyes, then cuts off its ears, and splits the head in half with a chopper and a coal hammer. It is horrible to watch. Into the big saucepan go the two halves of the head and it boils for hours and hours on the hob.

When everything has gone to pulp, including brains, Gran tips out the mess on to the big blue meat dish and takes out all the little bones and gristle. The kitchen is full of pig's head steam so I go outside and bang my clothes to get rid of the smell. Gran chops up everything very small and puts it into a mixing bowl to set in its own jelly, with a board and flat iron on top to press it down.

Gran's brawn is famous. My aunties even come up from Cwm to taste the stuff, but I can't stand it. I don't even fancy the orange.

*Essay from 'Oh My Life' published by Honno in 1988*

# The Row

Just risen from sleep
in its corrugated sheets and brass bedsteads,
the Row staggers along the mountain,
its unwashed face grey with yesterday's grime

In his garden,
Mr. Davies grows dandelions through rusty pushchairs,
,,,,,,,,,,,,,,,,,,,,,,,,,,,,,,,,tyres
,,,,,,,,,,,,,,,,,,,,,,,,,,,,,,,,eggshells
,,,,,,,,,,,,,,,,,,,,,,,,,,,,,,,,a pink lace corset
,,,,,,,,,,,,,,,,,,,,,,,,,,,,,,,,ashes and old daps.

Under a gooseberry bush, behind the coal cwch,
Elsie Hutchins and Cy Jones make love.
There will be jam when the harvest ripens,
spread on a new batch from the Co-op
or a bun from the oven,
with too many mouths to feed.

In the dry-ash closet of number one
Jackey Johnson sits
marking his coupon with indelible noughts and crosses.
In this sanctuary from his strict Baptist wife,
he prays to the great God Littlewood,
to bless him with a cheque for £10,000.
On the wooden seat,
he flies to Las Vegas and Monte Carlo,
and spins fantasies of Roulette, Baccarat,
Strip Jack Naked and loaded dice.

'Making your will up there, are you?'
The cold water voice, flung out of the kitchen,
dashes his dreams.

Children suck the edge of the table in number eight,
eyes wide, watching her bread-sharp knife
circling sour apples, dropping lover's names.

She wipes her hands on a pinny,
stretched tightly over her middle,
like pastry over pregnant lumps of apple.
A kiss of sugar then
to sweeten a satisfying tart.

Bronwen Parry, last house,
usherette to the palatial New Plaza,
looks in the fly-marked mirror
nailed over the soap dish
and pinches her finger waves, set with Amami,
the image of Ginger Rogers, or perhaps Alice Faye.

Mr. Jenkins
fights for breath.
with failing strength, hammers segs into shoes,
wishing he could patch his leather lungs.

On the corner, gangs of kids wait
for Maggie to come home from the Club.
They circle
and she picks up her frayed black skirts,
until her pink bloomers show,
and dances

*Colliers Row.*

*Sunday School Outing to Barry Island at Ebbw Vale Station reproduced with kind permission of Mr. & Mrs. M. Hodgson.*

# Red Swimming Costume

I ran home from chapel with a wet-week face.
There was no place for me
on the free trip to Barry,
I had no costume to go in the sea.

'Don't you worry' said Mam,
knew just what to do,
'Knit you one in a hurry, I will,
good as new; well nearly so.
Here's wool from a jumper, bought in Nantyglo
by your Aunty Ade.
Tuppence in a jumble sale she paid,
'Not my colour, it isn't' she said,
'I always look washed out in red'.'

Mam unravelled every row,
knotted short pieces,
I watched the ball grow.
Her needles clicked and in a day it was done
and none more pleased than me,
to swim with the chapel in the sea.

It had built-up shoulders to match my vest,
worn underneath not to catch cold,
and little legs with initials bold -
spelled out 'I...T'. 'IT'. Well I thought I was.

It was knitted in plain and knitted in pearl.
I gave a twirl before the glass,
admired my front and then my back
Mam had a knack of knitting allright.
It clung to my body really tight,

Though I didn't have much of an elegant figure,
when I grew old,
I would be bigger around the chest -
I thought that 48 bust would be best.

Before the great day I lay awake,
but in the morning made a mistake,
left off my vest to be like the rest.
Put the costume on, next to my skin.
I paid for my sin.

The wool made me itch as I sat in the train,
watching driving sheets of rain,
I gave a scratch and then a twitch.
It pricked and tickled.

I couldn't keep still,
Until Mam told me off, said she felt ill
watching me fidget, seeing me fuss,
threatened she'd send me back by bus.

I forgot about my agony when
I dived under the water into the sea,
which sucked the wool quite playfully.
Then it went cold - we were told to come out.
I stood on the sand, heavy as lead.
Someone saw me and shouted, threw back his head,
'Take a look there, at the IT girl,' he said.
The legs hung down, initials over my knee,
two pimples out for all to see.
My chest was bare.
All the chapel seemed to stare.

Looked down at myself, saw a knot unravel,
and a hole opened up and showed my navel.
Red dye flowed down my legs and feet.
I was coloured bright red, like a boiled-up beet.

Before I could utter one small vowel;
go and cover myself with a towel,
a photographer took a snap of me.
I left the sea, walked round the fair,
saw some people screaming there.
Pinned on a board for all to see,

there was the photograph of me,
exposed on the beach, and under developed.

Now when I see that photograph,
bought by my sister for a laugh,
I go hot and the colour starts to flow.
I remember the place where my pimples showed
and I dyed and went red in the face.

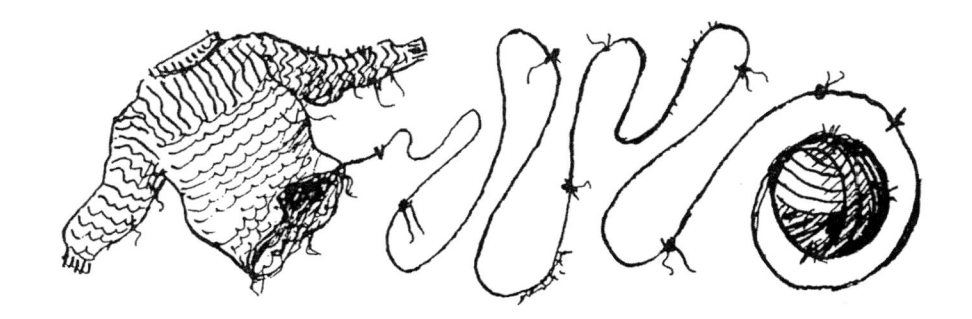

# Auntie May

Looking up, I searched for her on Saturdays,
a speck on the shoulder of Mynydd Carn y Cefn,
sweeping down the hill
between Sixth and Seventh Rows,
and across the valley to our kitchen,
which she filled with laughter-come-to-crying.

Smart as the catalogue ladies I cut out for fun,
she queened it in coloured beads and real diamanté.
I listened, all pigs ears,
while she poured out a stream of jokes with her tea,
and chewed on stories about budgies,
God, and her neighbours in Limestone Road.
My six year-old sides split and I had stitches.

Come Christmas, she gave me a 'whoopee' cushion
and a six-inch nail labelled, 'coat hanger'.
Filled a black woollen stocking for Gran
with coal, a packet of lard
and a square of Recketts Blue from the pantry.
Every Year Gran was surprised.

Auntie May came to my wedding,
in a jumble sale hat
perked with a spray of Woolworth's feathers,
squirming round a stalk.
Stuck in at an awkward angle,
they made me feel uncomfortable.

Lipstick ran into cracks around her mouth
and laughter lines cried in a parched pink foundation.
Her mauve chiffon scarf, tied in a kittenish bow,
clashed with loud yellow of her cardigan.
The gaudy beads rattled.

She pulled at my clothes,
wanting to tell me the same old jokes
I smiled politely.

# Picking

When there was no more school
and the sun had stayed out for two weeks.
Whinberries covered Mynydd Carn y Cefn
proud as the carpet in Auntie Beat's front room,
ankle deep and untrodden.
Gran sat like a queen
under her beehive hat minding the string-handled jars,
while workers brought her berries to pick over.

The skylark sang its vertical song
and pale moths disturbed from sleep
in White Ladies Bedstraw,
fluttered to rest
on leaves burned by the gawping sun.

The steamy finger of the long feeder below,
pointed rudely to the stripping
and rolling into sheets.

We sat in the Gods
with the navy blue knobs in the jars,
stained with royal purple
and blackened teeth, on edge against the grit.

We trailed home,
to hot whinberry tart from the side oven,
crisp, sugared and set in skintight custard.
Back to the clinker and ash of Gantre,
to pick a harder fruit.

# Telling the Runes

She regularly doled out a serving of six.
Swallowing hard,
I sucked the black swollen skins
and laid out hard cores
on the curved edge of the dish.
Gran told the runes,
but the prophecy was always the same,
one too many came to 'Poor Man'.

More pinch and scrape, turning the knife in pots
over barren seeds of raspberry
or smears of salmon and shrimp.
This glass was not clear,
but still we cast about for fortune
in sand, tea and Devil's cards.
Looked for diamonds in dregs
and a dark man with a ring of gold.

We had no need of Tinker or Tailor,
did our own mending and cutting out.
The solitary iron bee in its wooden hive,
hummed every evening
and Gran kept time on the treadle with her foot,
while its steel tongue licked shimmies into shape.

We counted soldiers, Albert next door,
a blancoed belt and spit and polish boots,
khaki rough as his tongue
and Iver, whose Navy collar we touched for luck,
but there was no future in it.

It never came to Beggar, that was too much.
'Feed your own' Gran maintained.

Hoping to take avoiding action,
I only ate five.

It did not work.

*Awarded The Oreil Book Prize 1990*

# Manmoel

Old enough,
I climbed Manmoel mountain to find the promised Dry Docks,
where ships sailed over the mountain from abroad.

Tree trunks on the edge of the mountain road,
bunched knotted knuckles, hard as miner's fists,
as if to throw down loaded dice on the Coal Board game
at Marine,
where a toy wheel turned, and leaden figures walked
among a layout of lines and loading sheds,
making signals and watching points.

Once, Old Coal, Threequarter and Big Vein
powered compound engines of battleships,
and fuelled the fires of war.

At the top, an ocean of wheat rolled and surged
under hills ankle-deep in whinberry.
Waves of song poured out from passengers in Paran chapel,
where old graves lay in ordered rows,
like boats in moorings, bows facing The Full Moon,
where men in drink lurched.

Water welled up at Ton Yr Efail Fach,
and the springs of Pen Rhiw Gyngi
filled the farmer's pool at Pen Rhiw Fawddog,
and on Pen y Fan Pond another child sailed a boat.

# Singer

The silver tongue was mute under the polished cover.
But when it saw daylight,
its song filled the dark corners of my childhood.

Golden scrolls feathered the sleek black body,
and its breast puffed out at the extravagance of the design.
This deep throated songster
moved to the rhythms of my grandmother's slippered foot,
dipping and rising on the iron lace of the treadle
and keeping time with her tuneless hum
of troubles packed up and how her heart was in Tipperary.
It was hard going when the tension grew too great
and the thread snapped, but she fed it through thick and thin
over sackcloth and white sheets turned to middle.
Nesting in its magpie drawer,
a collection of spindles and shuttles,
darners and pitted thimbles, a Newey Wizard bodkin,
and a linen tape to measure growing pains.
Pins in pink paper,
a gift from the Emporium instead of farthing change,
an amber bead and an army button dying for Brasso.

When its voice grew hoarse, it was well-oiled
and glided over binders, christening gowns
and Whitsun fine feathers.
Its foot hopped over seams and joins
as I did over cracked paving.
It was silent as war was declared,
but this bird-in-hand was brought into service,
made-do and mended, blind-stitched over blackout,
and flew over parachute silk, a cold skin clinging to a body.

When the beating was finished,
it was out of action and laid in the glory hole.

Afterwards it was sold for a song.

*Embroidery Collage on display in The County Hall, Cwmbran.*

# Winter Wash

The iron grip of winter held them fast.
Rinsed in Arctic water,
they hung over Ice-plant and Snow-on-the-mountain,
rigid as the whalebone in Gran's grey corset.
Pegged out, they were stiff as icicles fringing back kitchens.
Sun-ray doyleys froze to cotton snowflakes,
and gloves had bitten fingers.
Felt jumpers, their chain mail stitches
twisted into steel cables.
Knitted patches on the garden plot bedspread
hardened under a blanket of frost.
Ice doubled and trebled the woolly weight of the crochet shawl.

Brought in,
we played with them before it was too late.
Danced around the kitchen, arms outstretched,
cold partners melting to our touch.
Trousers stood leg-less, went weak at the knees.
We laughed most at Gran's long drawers,
sitting up by themselves on the arm chair,
sagging slowly as they felt the fire.

After dark, sheets, blown out by the north wind,
sailed in on a tide of cold air,
Sunlight Soap and Reckitts Blue.
They thawed in a crosswind from baking Welshcakes.

*Published by Pont Books
in 'Second Thoughts'.*

# ···· Additional Poems ····

## Faith

It is a wild bird,
which cannot be held with clenched fists,
or caged between the bars of creed and dogma.
It is not locked in masonry or stained glass,
but must have space to spread its wings and soar,
to touch the wings of angels.

Sometimes, there is no song,
I look up and see an empty sky,
then in the darkest hour,
it sings of resurrection and of hope.
In the long winter, when the body of the earth is cold,
suddenly it comes with bright eye and warmth in the breast
to comfort and to cheer.

For those who believe, it comes at a call
and sits as if it is on the right hand of God,
to feed on the natural Eucharist
of bread and water.

Sometimes I lose sight in the darkness of disbelief,
but I know that it is there.
It is the Great Owl,
seeing further than I am able in the gloom.
It is the eagle,
bearing me up when I take a leap
and my fledgeling wings are uncertain.
It is the dove
whose flight-feathers can soar to love
and return with the promise of The Holy Spirit.

It is the sparrow which tells me I am counted.

# Angels

In space,
God put angels to whisper and inspire.
They hovered in my childhood dreams,
while I slept bolstered with goose feathers.
and they cradled my head with wings.
When I lay awake and was afraid, they shielded me from devils,
dodging and quivering in the light of the candle flame
flickering on white-washed walls.
Outside my safety barrier of iron bars and brass bed-knobs
they guarded dark corners
and filled the bottomless stair-well with Halleluahs.

In their gilded and moulded frames,
they blew trumpets loud enough for God to hear in heaven,
and promised salvation for
Good Attendance, Baptism and Temperance.
On the gold edged pages of the Bible,
sharp as the tongue of Ezekiel,
their feathers filled the finely etched skies
over Bethlehem and Golgotha.

Pages turned, and I lost sight of them in black holes.
I set up angels of my own,
poor ghosts without voice or chains to rattle.
Looked for comfort at the spit and polish brass angel
bearing up the Bible in St. John's,
but in her face there was no joy or recognition.

Now, I know that they do not need wings,
or hands to hold.
Their substance is firer than bone or feather.
They have the power of one whose arms were lifted up,
and nailed against the stars.

# Stained Glass

As fragile as a May-fly's wing,
yet weathering the winds of heaven.

River sand and beechwood ash,
fused by fire and stained,
an ancient art of alchemy,
secrets kept.

In church and chancel, cloister and cathedral,
glaziers laboured with grozers and shears,
stopping knives and lathekins
hammered fire into stone,
giving a greater vision.

Images of saints in true colours,
passed through flame,
their auras glow with spiritual fire,
ruby, amber and amethyst.

Fish netted into cobalt seas,
waves stilled with calms.
Bird, leaf and butterfly,
intensify in inner darkness.

Base metal comes between pieces of God,
and fragments of angels,
in the eye of the Dean at Lincoln.
Shaped in a different setting,
Adam and Eve walk with leaden feet,
away from a rose-coloured garden.
Flaws and grits, made in human error,
have value as a means to light.

Man can look at moon and see himself,
but in that moment when illumination comes,
the light of Spirit is too bright.
Yet between the blindness and the sight,
there is a screen, and looking up, through tinted glass,
he sees the ultimate design.

# Search For a Garden

Shackled with the chains of motion sickness,
I have not seen the Hanging Gardens,
or warmed my cold Welsh bones in Caribbean sun.
Yet between these mountains,
I have travelled a million miles.

Searching for Eden, I stumbled on stony paths,
burdened with the back pack of self doubt.
Dandelion clocks marked time
and their seeds spiralled into air,
like my prayers for inner peace
and a pleasant place to rest.

So far,
I have not found the garden,
but on the way, have seen the promise of the Gardener
in the red amphitheatre of the poppy,
where bees perform their pollen dances;
in the yellow trumpet of the daffodil
blowing out its cheeks to herald Spring,
and in hedgerows filled with Traveller's Joy.

# Acknowledgements

To my friends Angela Savage and Gillian Clarke, poets and teachers who encouraged and helped me when I first started to write poetry. They gave me faith and encouragement in those early days.

Angela wanted me to write some spiritual poetry, so I hope she would have approved of the ones I have included here as an addition to the main theme.

The poem 'Teachers Marks' is dedicated to Miss Stevens, a teacher in Pontygof Girls School. She paid for me to join the library at the Institute when I was nine, so that I would have books to read. Also thanks to my friend Mandy Bidgway, for her help and interest.

Paintings and sketches by Irene E. Thomas.